Backya Bird watching

36 AUSTRALIAN BIRDS TO ENJOY

Share magic moments in nature

Ron Smith OAM and Bob Winters

Dedicated to the preservation of the environment of Australia's Backyards

Published by Wilkinson Publishing Pty Ltd
ACN 006 042 173
PO Box 24135, Melbourne, VIC 3001, Australia
Ph: +61 3 9654 5446
enquiries@wilkinsonpublishing.com.au
www.wilkinsonpublishing.com.au

Photography by Bob Winters.
Cover and book design by Tango Media.
Printed in China.

ISBN: 9781922810502

A catalogue record for this book is available from the National Library of Australia

A catalogue record for this book is available from the National Library of Australia.

Follow Wilkinson Publishing on social media.

 WilkinsonPublishing

 wilkinsonpublishinghouse

 WPBooks

Share your bird snaps with us!
www.backyardbirdwatching.com.au

CONTENTS

QUICK BIRD INDEX

INTRODUCTION

Wherever you are outdoors, you will find birds. These are fascinating creatures whose ancient ancestors were feathered dinosaurs.

Birds will make their homes in our gardens and even in our busiest cities. The more natural the environment the more kinds of birds you will find.

There are many hundreds of birds in Australia, but only some live in our garden. This book will help you enjoy your garden birds and be captivated by their spellbinding behaviours.

Birds have many things in common. They are covered in feathers which help them fly and keep them warm. Did you know their body temperature is higher than ours? They have beaks and wings and walk on their toes. Their eggs have a hard shell and need to be kept warm.

Birds lay their eggs in nests. Most birds look after their hatchlings. They either feed their chicks or show them where to find food.

Wilbur Worm, environmental educator, is a constant bird watcher.

10 TIPS FOR BIRDWATCHING

#1: Look for movement
Our eyes are very good at seeing movement. Look in the tree, bushes and on the ground for movement. Don't forget to look at the sky for flying birds. It is harder to see moving birds on windy days. Even colourful parrots are hard to spot when they are still.

#2: Look in the direction of calling birds
Our ears are good at pinpointing the location of where a sound is coming from. Keep searching in the direction of the call until you find the bird.

#3: Look for birds at different times of the day
Some birds are most active at dawn and dusk. Other birds move between different gardens. On hot days, birds will often rest in the middle of the day. You will find more birds if you look for them at different times.

#4: Learn to use binoculars
Many birds will not allow you to get close to them. Binoculars are used to see the details of birds. Ask an adult to help you learn how to use binoculars.

#5: When watching birds, move slowly or not at all
Birds are very good at picking up movement. Compared to a bird you are very large. When you move towards birds, there will be a distance when they feel in danger and will fly away.

#6: Don't point

When bird watching with other people, it is very tempting to point where the bird is. If you are close to a bird and point with an outstretched arm it will look like something dangerous is moving towards it and it will fly away.

#7: Find something helpful to identify birds

This book will help you identify the most common birds in your garden. There are many books, posters, brochures and online resources that can help you identify some of the other birds that might visit.

#8: Make a list of the birds you see

Once you have identified a bird in your garden add it to a list. You might want to learn more about the bird by reading this book, other books or looking it up on the internet.

#9: Document what the birds are doing

Write down or draw a picture of what the birds are doing. Don't forget to also record the date and time of day.

#10: Learn the different calls each type of bird makes

Most kinds of birds have their own call. Try to learn what calls each makes. Some people are good at copying bird calls. Try to copy the bird calls you hear and the birds might answer back.

WHERE BIRDS LIVE IN YOUR GARDEN

Tree tops: Many small to large birds feed and rest in the leafy canopy of trees.

Tree trunks and branches: Birds search the branches and trunks of trees for insects and spiders. They might sit on a branch while they search the ground, tree or air for prey. Most birds sit on branches to rest and sleep.

In the bushes: Many smaller birds feed and hide in bushes. Dense prickly bushes are the best place for smaller birds to hide from danger.

Under bushes: The damp softer soil and leaf litter can be a good place for birds to scratch around for a feed.

Garden bed: Ground feeding birds like to seek worms, insects and spiders in garden beds. Some birds will be searching for seeds.

Among the mulch and compost heap: Wherever plants and leaves are decomposing, there will be a lot of insect and worm food for birds to eat.

Lawn: Only a few birds will find food on your lawn. Most of these will be introduced pests.

Flying high: Birds fly between places and hunt from the air or catch flying insects. Some birds even show off to their mates by flying acrobatics. Always keep an eye on the sky.

Bird baths and water features: Birds will find water in your garden to drink and bath.

Look for surprises around places like the garden shed: Bird nests can be hidden away in all kinds of strange places.

Roof, TV aerial, gutters and power lines: There are many things that people have built where birds can rest and watch out for danger. Being up high and in the open makes it harder for hunters to sneak up.

LEARNING TO USE BINOCULARS

Find the three adjustments: To use binoculars it is best to first learn how to adjust them. Most binoculars have three different adjustments.

Zero the eye piece: One of the two eye pieces on the binoculars will rotate. This adjustment helps people who usually wear glasses. Most people need to have this eye piece set to zero.

Adjust the two barrels: The binoculars bend in the middle so the two barrels can be adjusted to suit the distance between the eyes. Bend the binoculars until it is easy to see through both barrels.

Focus: To focus the binoculars, most have a small rotating wheel in the middle between the two barrels. Move the wheel both ways until the thing you are looking at is in focus.

Improve your skills: Next is developing the skill to point the binoculars and find the bird or thing you wish to look at.

Use the binocular straps: It is best to keep the binocular straps around your neck.

Cleaning: Only use a lens cleaning cloth or very clean cotton hanky to clean the lenses.

Protection: Make sure the binoculars never get wet. Do not drop the binoculars.

GALAH

Size:	Large, 37cm long.
Where they hang out:	Large flocks of Galahs live around farming country, in country towns, on golf courses and parks. Small groups or larger flocks might also visit your garden.
What they get up to:	Galahs have short legs, so they waddle along the ground in search of seeds. When they climb around trees eating seeds, flowers or berries they can use their curved beak to hang onto branches. They can form exceptionally large noisy flocks. Early in the morning they might swoop high over the trees before deciding where to head for their daily feed. Many Galahs make a big racket, but unlike children, as soon as it's dark they are sound asleep and silent. When flying at dawn and dusk the pink and grey colours of Galahs are highlights in the landscape.
Conservation:	Galahs need hollows in old trees to nest and often return to the same stand of trees each evening to sleep.

SULPHUR-CRESTED COCKATOO

Size:	Large, 47cm long.
Where they hang out:	These cockatoos gather at night to roost in the top of large gum trees. They feed in large flocks or spread out. Thousands may be seen feeding on farmland paddocks. Smaller numbers of groups call our cities home.
What they get up to:	Sulphur-crested Cockatoos are known for their piercing screech as they fly and perch in trees. Most of their feeding is on the ground. As they waddle on their short legs, they find seeds, bulbs and insects to eat. In trees they also eat flowers and berries. Their strong beaks can crack nuts, shred bark and renovate tree hollows for nesting. Their bright yellow crest is used to communicate with other cockatoos.
Conservation:	If you do not want to share your fruit trees with cockatoos, you may need to put a net over the tree. Large flocks of cockatoos can damage newly sown crops.

CRIMSON ROSELLA

Size:	Large, 35cm long.
Where they hang out:	Crimson Rosellas can be seen high up in the canopy of gum trees or down on the ground. They are most common in wet forests. They often visit native gardens and picnic areas. They need large tree hollows to nest in.
What they get up to:	These Rosellas have many different calls to stay in communication with their friends. They mostly eat seeds and flowers. While feeding in trees, you might see bits of nuts and flowers raining down. Their hooked beak is an excellent nutcracker. Even though their colour is dazzling, they are very difficult to spot when they are motionless in a tree. They are often in small flocks. Young Crimson Rosellas are mostly green with only some blue and crimson.
Conservation:	Only old, large trees will have big enough tree hollows for their nests. People can provide nesting boxes for them in their gardens.

RAINBOW LORIKEET

Size:	Medium, 29cm long.
Where they hang out:	Any kind of flowering native tree in a forest can be home to Rainbow Lorikeets. The more native plants we put in our gardens the more Lorikeets will visit.
What they get up to:	You will see small flocks of these parrots rocketing overhead while screeching to their mates. Like Honeyeaters, Lorikeets also have a brushy tongue for licking pollen and nectar from flowers. They eat fruit and will also eat seeds. You will hear them chatter as they feed. Rainbow Lorikeets might look attractive, but they are very aggressive to other kinds of birds feeding in trees or when they want to own a tree hollow for nesting. They could have also been called Noisy Lorikeets.
Conservation:	Rainbow Lorikeets have become common garden birds as people grow more native plants like this grevillea. They will use your bird bath.

MUSK LORIKEET

Size:	Medium, 28cm long.
Where they hang out:	They spend nearly all their time in the canopies of eucalypts.
What they get up to:	These lorikeets seem to know where the best flowing gums and some of their favourite shrubs are. They feed in flocks, often with other nectar feeding birds. Their brushy tongue gathers flower pollen and nectar. The pollen that sticks to their face will help pollinate other trees. They aren't always noisy and their green feathers make them hard to spot in the tops of trees. Watch as they climb around the branches poking their beaks into the flowers. They are fast flyers, making a racket as they swiftly pass overhead.
Conservation:	Musk Lorikeets prefer tree hollows with a small entrance to squeeze through. Many of the gum varieties in our gardens and parks provide lorikeets with extra food throughout the year.

NANKEEN KESTREL

Size:	Large, 33cm long.
Where they hang out:	You might see them on power lines, on the guttering of your home, in a tree or swooping past. They like to be near open ground where they do most of their hunting. They only hit the ground when there is a chance of catching some food.
What they get up to:	They will often face the wind and with strong wing beats hover about 30 metres above the ground. When they see a large insect, mouse or lizard they will dive and snatch the prey with sharp, curved talons. The Kestrels' curved beak is used to shred their prey into small strips that can be swallowed. When one arrives in your garden, many of the other birds will screech their warning calls and some of them may pester the Kestrel.
Conservation:	Kestrels will hang around towns and homes if they are not harassed by people or their pets.

TAWNY FROGMOUTH

Size:	Large, 45cm long.
Where they hang out:	They are mostly seen during the day sitting motionless on a large tree limb. At night they hunt. They need large trees to perch in and make a nest in a fork.
What they get up to:	Tawny Frogmouths' camouflage helps them look like part of the limb they are perched on. You may only know they are nearby when they call at night, making a low 'oom oom' call. When hunting at night, they silently fly like a ghost. They use their wide mouth to snap up large insects, mice, frogs and other small animals living on the ground. They can also catch moths caught in a car's headlights. They have large yellow eyes for seeing in the dark. Their very cute chicks are white fluffy balls.
Conservation:	Many frogmouths become roadkill due to them hunting along country roads.

KOOKABURRA

Size:	Large, 45cm long.
Where they hang out:	They spend most of their life perched on horizontal branches, preferably without many leaves. Their nest is a tree hollow.
What they get up to:	Their laughing song is used to maintain their territory from neighbouring Kookaburras. Laughing is done by the entire family. Kookaburra chicks stay with the family even after they leave the nest. They will help to feed future chicks. Kookaburras patiently sit on a perch waiting for a meal to appear. They use their powerful beak to clamp onto lizards, mice, insects, frogs and many other animals. They give their food a good beating against a branch before they eat it. It takes a lot of effort to hop on their short legs when they are on the ground.
Conservation:	Kookaburras need at least one suitable hole as part of their territory. In gardens, pet cats eat most of the Kookaburra's food.

LITTLE RAVEN

Size:	Large, 50cm long.
Where they hang out:	They rest in treetops and feed on the ground. They make a messy nest of sticks high up in trees. Ravens are seen in public areas like school grounds.
What they get up to:	There are several types of birds that are called Crows and Ravens and they are difficult to tell apart. These black birds are considered to be some of the most intelligent birds. The Little Raven is only a tiny bit smaller than other Ravens. They are noisy when flying. Pairs of Little Ravens keep other Ravens out of their territory when breeding. Following this breeding they gather in large flocks. They eat up any food that is available, so they help to keep our environment clean and reduce the number of small pest animals. Their diet includes large dead animals such as roadkill.
Conservation:	Ravens are great at helping the environment and farmers by eating pest animals.

AUSTRALIAN MAGPIE

Size:	Large, 40cm long.
Where they hang out:	They prefer to rest in trees or on fence posts or power lines. Feeding is on the ground, usually out in the open. It seems our gardens are to their liking.
What they get up to:	Magpies sing or carol in family groups to maintain their territory. Long legs help them walk with a long stride. Their powerful beak has a fine point that can delicately pick up the tiniest insect or spider. Count how often they peck the ground. They mate for life and maintain a strict territory while breeding. The nest is a messy platform of sticks high up in a tree. A few individual magpies will attack during the breeding season starting in late winter. The individual Magpie usually has a special target. It is often cyclists, sometimes it is cats, it could be walkers or even the postie on their bike.
Conservation:	Pet cats pose the greatest danger to Magpies in our gardens.

MAGPIE-LARK

Size:	Medium to large, 28cm long.
Where they hang out:	They will be seen resting in trees and power lines or even on the veranda rail of homes. They feed on the ground, roadside and along the water's edge. They don't like long grass.
What they get up to:	Magpie-larks are one of three types of birds that make their nest from just mud. The nest is like a round, hollowed out mudbrick glued onto a horizontal branch. They feed on small insects, spiders and worms on the ground or water's edge. As they walk their head jerks on their skinny neck. What really happens is the head stays still as the body moves and then the head is jerked forward to catch up with the body. Males and females sing together. The male calls followed by the female making a different call. It sounds like 'Peewee'.
Conservation:	Pet cats pose the greatest danger to Magpie-larks in our gardens.

PIED CURRAWONG

Size:	Large, 46cm long.
Where they hang out:	During the spring and summer they breed in the mountains. For winter they head for the lowlands and many visit our gardens and parks. Currawongs need some large trees to rest in and are happy to feed in trees or on the ground. However, Currawongs are now starting to breed in the lowlands because more food is available.
What they get up to:	Currawongs will form flocks when they are not breeding. Their loud, tuneful call can be heard over long distances as they fly. They protect the forests by eating thousands of stick insects. Around our homes and parks, they will eat berries, insects, lizards, small birds and even dead rotting animals. Both male and females gather materials for the nest, but the female builds it. While the female incubates the eggs, the male will feed her.
Conservation:	In your garden they might be eating any nesting chicks they find.

WILLIE WAGTAIL

Size:	Small, 20cm long.
Where they hang out:	They will always be close to branches where they can rest, watch out for food and launch themselves into the air. Wagtails will also hop along the ground.
What they get up to:	While they rest on a branch, Wagtails watch out for flying insects and movement on the ground. When a flying insect is spotted, they dart and weave after it, snapping the insect up in its beak. Their tail is always wagging. Wagtails can be very brave. They often attack much larger birds they think could be a threat, even an eagle more than 100 times their weight. Some Wagtails will join you when you are gardening to find the insects you disturb. They will sit on the back of a sheep or kangaroo, waiting for insects to be disturbed.
Conservation:	They don't have any known conservation problems and seem to be able to survive in the most extraordinary places.

GREY BUTCHERBIRD

Size:	Medium, 28cm long.
Where they hang out:	Butcherbirds spend most of the day perched on a branch carefully studying the ground, trees and bushes around them for large items of food.
What they get up to:	The Butcherbird's song is one of the favourites of many people interested in birds. They eat large insects, lizards, baby birds and even mice. From their perch they pounce on their prey. Their powerful hooked beak is used for clamping onto and crushing their prey. When they feel full, they will keep hunting. Any new prey they catch will be hung in a tree for later. That is why they are called Butcherbirds. They are fearless defending their nest, attacking any intruder. However they steal chicks from other birds' nests.
Conservation:	Domestic cats will eat most of the Butcherbird's food. They can't survive once forests are cleared.

BLACK-FACED CUCKOO-SHRIKE

Size:	Medium, 36cm long.
Where they hang out:	They live in most places in Australia provided there are some large trees. Only some migrate.
What they get up to:	You will soon learn to identify the chirping call of the Cuckoo-shrike. They sit high in trees or sometimes on power lines spying for anything moving on the ground or in trees. They eat creatures among the leaves and branches. They can catch flying insects. They dive on ground animals from their perch. Their flight is smooth but lazy and undulating as they glide after several wingbeats. Cuckoo-shrikes nest with the same mate each year. They raise two chicks in their small cup-shaped nest. They are not Cuckoos. Cuckoos lay their eggs in other birds' nest, obliging these birds to raise their chicks.
Conservation:	They need forests and trees to perch in.

CRESTED PIGEON

Size:	Medium to large, 33cm long.
Where they hang out:	These native pigeons are often found in parks and open areas. They are common along country roads and on power lines. They are becoming more common in our gardens.
What they get up to:	Crested Pigeons are mostly seen in small flocks. They spend much of the day feeding on the ground. All pigeons use their short narrow beaks like a pair of tweezers to pick up seeds from the ground. The seeds are ground up by their crop, a muscle where the food is stored, before entering their stomach. They run along the ground on their short legs. When Crested Pigeons take off, their wings make a loud whistling sound. They bob their head up and down as they display with their mate. If they make a nest in your garden, it will only be a few sticks resting on some branches.
Conservation:	They can become victims to cats.

SPOTTED TURTLE-DOVE

Size:	Medium to large, 31cm long.
Where they hang out:	Turtle Doves will be seen resting in trees and feeding on the ground. They are most common around homes.
What they get up to:	These birds were introduced from overseas. They are native to Asia. Their presence seems to reduce the number of some native pigeons. While most ground feeding pigeons eat seed, Turtle Doves eat a lot of pet food or any other food left out. They can breed during most of the year. Some people find their constant cooing annoying. There is no scientific difference between different types of pigeons and doves. Often smaller pigeons are called doves.
Conservation:	These feral birds compete with our native pigeons. Keep your pet food inside where these doves can't eat it.

FERAL PIGEON

Size:	Large, 34cm long.
Where they hang out:	Large numbers are found in our cities. Massive flocks circle our suburbs. They are found in our towns and covering our wheat silos. They roost on the sides of our city buildings and under bridges.
What they get up to:	This species is also known as Rock Doves, domestic pigeons, racing pigeons, homing pigeons and flying rats. They have many different colour patterns. Some have been bred to grow fancy feathers. On city streets, they get under our feet. They swarm around us as we eat in urban parks. They nest on ledges on buildings and nest hollows. They are like a plague in most of the world's cities. In our cities there are falcons that will eat the pigeons and their squabs (pigeon chicks).
Conservation:	Their messy poo eats into the world's most important buildings and monuments causing billions of dollars of damage and repairs. To reduce their numbers, people should not feed them.

RUFOUS WHISTLER

Size:	Small, 17mm long.
Where they hang out:	They are usually seen in eucalypt trees. They find small creatures among the bark of trees and large shrubs. They come down to bathe and drink.
What they get up to:	The photo is of the male Rufous Whistler. The female is plain with dark streaks. At the start of the breeding season, the males establish their territory with loud outbursts of their loud tuneful song. Every time one male starts others follow. If you can repeat the start of their whistle, it will generate a frenzy of song from all the other birds. Even a sharp sound will get an instant reply. After a few weeks, the whistlers get busy nesting and reduce their whistling challenges with the opposing birds.
Conservation:	As we plant more gum trees in our gardens, we can expect more whistlers.

EASTERN SPINEBILL

Size:	Small, 16cm long.
Where they hang out:	They will be found in flowering bushes and some garden plants with tubular flowers. Spinebills like dense bushes so they can escape the larger and more aggressive Honeyeater cousins.
What they get up to:	Spinebill's long, curved bill is perfect for probing tubular flowers where they collect pollen and nectar with their brushy tongue. They feed on most flowers at shrub level. Spinebills are busy feeding all day moving from flower to flower. As adults they mostly eat from flowers and take some insects. However, they catch insects to feed their chicks. When you see a Spinebill grasping an insect, you know it's feeding its young.
Conservation:	They feed on the many flowering native plants in our garden. They are preyed on by cats. Noisy Miners, which are increasing in numbers, constantly harass smaller Honeyeaters. Planting dense prickly bushes allows Spinebills to escape from larger birds.

WHITE-PLUMED HONEYEATER

Size:	Small, 16cm long.
Where they hang out:	The favoured home of White-plumed Honeyeaters is River Red Gum forests. They do live over much of Australia and have taken a liking to our native gardens. They are mostly seen zipping around the tops of gum trees. They will come down to feed on flowers and insects.
What they get up to:	They usually feed in large groups. Their load call can easily be heard indoors. They fly like tiny speeding darts zipping in and out of tree canopies. These Honeyeaters spend all day feeding and swooping about after flying insects. They also chase each other and other Honeyeaters. They have a long brushy tongue for licking pollen and nectar from flowers. They also search for insects and spiders in the tree canopy and tree trunk.
Conservation:	They will visit any garden or location with a gum tree, even in the middle of a city where one gum tree stands.

NEW HOLLAND HONEYEATER

Size:	Small, 18cm long.
Where they hang out:	The New Holland Honeyeater loves the flowering bushes in heathland, along the coast and under forest canopies. They seem to have become the most common Honeyeater in our gardens.
What they get up to:	There are normally a few of them feeding together. They can be described as hyperactive. When they are not feeding on flowers, they use their skilful acrobatics to catch flying insects, squabbling and chasing each other and checking out every nook and cranny among the shrubs and trees. They never seem to sit still. They move around finding the best flowering plants, taking claim of the bounty. Once in your garden, they will make themselves at home and will come quite close as you quietly potter about.
Conservation:	They like our native gardens. We need to preserve the understory of forest and the heathlands. They will enjoy a garden bird bath.

SINGING HONEYEATER

Size:	Small, 20cm long.
Where they hang out:	They are found over much of Australia, except the east coast, but that could change. It's amazing how often they are seen while travelling around Australia. They prefer to feed in shrubs.
What they get up to:	Singing Honeyeaters are often seen alone. That's why you might not think they are common. Feeding in shrubs and low down in trees, they seek out insects and spiders and feed on the flowers. These Honeyeaters will even feed on the ground. They are easily spotted by looking in the direction of their singing call. Much larger Pallid Cuckoos will remove one of the Honeyeater's eggs and lay their own in its place. The parents will then raise the chick. As it grows, it looks like a large monster compared with its adopted parents.
Conservation:	The understory of our forests and plants in our arid zones need to be protected.

RED WATTLEBIRD

Size:	Medium, 34cm long.
Where they hang out:	They spend most of their time in flowering gums or other flowering plants. They love gardens with native flowering plants and large gum trees.
What they get up to:	Red Wattlebirds are one of the most common garden birds once gum trees have been planted. When they are not eating nectar from flowers or eating insects, they chase other birds from their favourite flowering trees. Their bird call is like putting together a cough and a dog bark—it's not pleasant. They are one of the first birds to wake up in the morning. They enjoy garden bird baths and then sitting on a branch and ruffling their feathers. When you see them in the dust on sunny days with their wings spread out, they are killing the bird lice in their feathers.
Conservation:	Red Wattlebirds are here to stay. Even cats find them hard to catch.

LITTLE FRIARBIRD

Size:	Medium, 28cm long.
Where they hang out:	They spend their lives in trees and shrubs but like to be close to water. Little Friarbirds live over half of Australia where there are waterways. Many home gardens meet their needs.
What they get up to:	When feeding, they are very busy leaping between flowers and shuffling their beak into them. They are happy to feed alone, with other friarbirds or other Honeyeaters. Like all Honeyeaters they use their brushy tongue to gather nectar and pollen from flowers. Insects and other small creatures are an important part of their diet. After heavy rain, Friarbirds move in to feast on the explosion of insects. In summer some of these birds move south while the rest stay behind. They prefer to make their delectate hanging nest over water. To spot them, listen out for their load 'ar-coo' call.
Conservation:	Provide a bird bath and keep domestic cats under control.

NOISY FRIARBIRD

Size:	Medium, 33cm long.
Where they hang out:	They are usually found up in the tree canopies of eucalypts and other trees heavy in flower. They are common in dry forests and woodlands.
What they get up to:	Noisy Friarbirds have a black featherless head so it is no wonder some people call them leather-heads. As the name suggests, it's a bird that can't shut up. They are noisiest in the morning and evening chattering away in the tree canopy. Noisy Friarbirds are at home in flowering trees rich in nectar. They are energetically climbing through the branches diligently probing the flowers. They're happy to feed in flocks and with Honeyeaters of a similar size. They persecute smaller Honeyeaters, constantly chasing them away. They also feed on insects and berries. They remain with the same mate when they breed each year.
Conservation:	Their forest home needs protection.

NOISY MINER

Size:	Medium, 27cm long.
Where they hang out:	They like to swoop through the tops of trees and dive into bushes. They will hop along the ground or along branches.
What they get up to:	Noisy Miners behave themselves in small groups but when in large gangs they bully other birds. They can also be annoying as they squawk all day. This helps them to keep together and tell other birds that they are the boss. If that wasn't bad enough, they farm lerps. These bugs suck sap from leaves and form a white sugar cap on their back. The miners eat the sugar and protect the lerps from other birds. They have been seen transferring lerps to other trees. After years of infestation the tree can die. They also eat nectar from flowers and insects and spiders.
Conservation:	Too many Noisy Miners stop other birds from eating some bugs so they become pests that can damage gum trees.

FIGBIRD

Size:	Medium, 28cm long.
Where they hang out:	They are a more tropical bird that will be seen in any trees with a crop of figs. They will also have a rest on power lines.
What they get up to:	Figbirds have a noisy chatter as they feed on figs, small fruits, flowers and insects. They will often gorge themselves in a fig tree until all the figs have run out. They like to hang out and feed with other Figbirds in small flocks of around 20. They even build their nests close together. These birds will perform all kinds of acrobatics to get to fruit or flowers. Where figs are planted in parks and gardens, they become popular with Figbirds. The photo is of a male Figbird. Females are brown and speckled and don't have a red face.
Conservation:	As long as we don't remove their main food trees, Figbirds will remain common.

SUPERB FAIRY-WREN

Size:	Small, 14cm long.
Where they hang out:	They are found in areas with dense undergrowth and bushes that hasn't been totally destroyed over a long time. They will happily feed in the open provided they can bounce back into cover.
What they get up to:	Fairy-wrens live in family groups. While the adults do the nesting duties the entire family feed and protect the younger chicks. There is one dominant male, but research has shown that neither the male nor female are always faithful. They feed among the ground cover and remain low among shrubs as their family group picks through the vegetation for insects, spiders and other tiny creatures. They use their call to stay in contact and maintain their territory while breeding. They join up with other flocks after the breeding season.
Conservation:	They do not migrate. Their ground cover of grass tussocks, bushes and even blackberries must be maintained. When this is done, they can even survive in city parks.

SILVEREYE

Size:	Small, 12cm long.
Where they hang out:	Tiny Silvereyes might be seen in the tops of trees and down into the lowest branches of bushes. During winter they form large flocks and head north.
What they get up to:	Small fluttering Silvereyes can be seen bobbing through the bushes in your garden and they enjoy splashing in your birdbath. They can gulp down quite large berries but they spend most of their time searching for insects and spiders. When they are not breeding, they are often seen with other small insect-eating birds. When conditions are good, they will raise a second or even third clutch of eggs. In winter, while Silvereyes in your garden have headed north, your garden might become home to Silvereyes from further down south.
Conservation:	Remove introduced garden plants with small red berries as Silvereyes might spread the seeds in the local bush and other people's gardens.

BROWN THORNBILL

Size:	Small, 10cm long.
Where they hang out:	They make their home in forests with a thick shrub layer. Gardens with native shrubby plants are good homes because they also provide insects and spiders which thornbills like to eat.
What they get up to:	In Australia there are many tiny brown birds which are hard to identify. The Brown Thornbill is one of these small birds more likely to visit your garden. Bird watchers listen for their musical call, their bright orange eye and streaky chest. Thornbills use their tiny beak to feed on insects and spiders that they peck from leaves and branches. Pairs of Brown Thornbills keep a small territory that they vigorously defend during the breeding season. In the colder months they join small flocks of other birds moving through the forest or through gardens.
Conservation:	The shrubby understory of forests and other environments need to be protected from mass destruction.

WELCOME SWALLOW

Size:	Small, 15cm long.
Where they hang out:	If they are not swooping around they will be resting on a branch, fence or any external part of your home.
What they get up to:	Swallows skilfully swoop, twist and dart around catching flying insects which they snap up with their wide-open beaks. When they are not breeding, they can form exceptionally large flocks. Hundreds may line up on power lines. When you see large numbers swirling high in the air, they are catching rising insects. The insects fly higher before a cold front hits. They often nest under eaves or under porches of homes where their nests are sheltered. Swallows tend to return each year. They make their nests from balls of mud which they stick on the wall.
Conservation:	If you don't like the swallows' droppings under their nests, glue or screw a tray under the nest to catch the droppings.

BLACKBIRD

Size:	Medium, 26cm long.
Where they hang out:	Blackbirds will be found under and in bushes, in garden beds and on the lawn. You might find their large mud and grass nests in a bush or garden shed.
What they get up to:	Blackbirds were brought from Europe and released in Australia. They attack some native birds and prevent them from being in our gardens. They also invade the bush. The photo is of a male Blackbird. You will see females are brown, not black. Each spring the males become aggressive with each other as they work out the boundaries of their territory. While they establish their territories, they sing at the crack of dawn and even at night. When feeding, they find a lot of small creatures along the edge of paths. As they dig away, you end up with soil on your paths.
Conservation:	It is best not to feed or encourage Blackbirds.

HOUSE SPARROW

Size:	Small, 15cm long.
Where they hang out:	They mostly live in our cities, around our homes and in many agricultural areas. At home, you will see them resting low in the bushes or on a fence, on the lawn or among the garden beds. Native gardens seem to have fewer sparrows compared to English-style gardens.
What they get up to:	House Sparrows make their dome-shaped nest wherever they can find a crevice. This could be in a brick wall, the side of a garden shed, the eaves or a crack in a tree. Many Sparrows nesting in the eaves of country homes will add to the fire risk if there is a bushfire. Sparrows form large flocks and are very noisy. They eat seeds and any food we leave lying around.
Conservation:	Never feed Sparrows. If Sparrows make their nests in eaves, an adult should remove nesting material and block the holes and crevices. In a bushfire, the nesting material might catch fire.

COMMON STARLING

Size:	Small to medium, 20cm long.
Where they hang out:	On farmland Starlings will form flocks of many thousands of birds. Hundreds can sleep in a single tree. They will sit on your roof and TV aerial as well as trees. Most of their feeding is on the ground.
What they get up to:	In Australia, these birds are introduced pests. In England, where they belong, they are disappearing. Starlings take over nesting hollows. They are dirty birds making the hollows so polluted and full of parasites that native parrots won't use the hollows. They also nest in eaves using grass for nesting material. This could catch fire during a bushfire.
Conservation:	Never feed Starlings. An adult should block up eaves where Starlings might try to nest. On the Nullabor plane, a team patrols the region to prevent Starlings from getting into Western Australia. The patrol uses dynamite to blow up the tree the starlings are sleeping in.

COMMON MYNA

Size:	Medium, 24cm long.
Where they hang out:	They often form large flocks. Mynas mostly feed on the ground. They are common around homes, cities, towns and farms. They will also live in the forests next to farmland. Flocks sleep together in the same trees each night.
What they get up to:	These birds were introduced into Australia and have become a pest. Mynas are very aggressive and bully many of the birds in your garden. Like Starlings they take over nest hollows and pollute them so badly native parrots can't use them. They also nest in eaves of homes. They are less common in the countryside than Starlings and prefer to stay near trees. They are very clever and can't be easily outsmarted by people.
Conservation:	Never feed Mynas and prevent them from eating your pet's food. An adult should block up eaves where Mynas might try to nest. Parking under their sleeping tree will cover the car in bird poop.

PHOTO CHECKLIST

Tick off the birds you've spotted!

☐ Galah

☐ Sulphur-crested Cockatoo

☐ Crimson Rosella

☐ Rainbow Lorikeet

☐ Musk Lorikeet

☐ Nankeen Kestrel

☐ Tawny Frogmouth

☐ Kookaburra

☐ Little Raven

☐ Australian Magpie

☐ Magpie-lark

☐ Pied Currawong

☐ Willie Wagtail

☐ Grey Butcherbird

☐ Black-faced Cuckoo-shrike

☐ Crested Pigeon